GIRLS WE HAVE KNOWN

AND OTHER ONE-ACT PLAYS

BY RALPH PAPE

DRAMATISTS
PLAY SERVICE
INC.

GIRLS WE HAVE KNOWN AND OTHER ONE-ACT PLAYS
Copyright © 1984, Ralph Pape

GIRLS WE HAVE KNOWN
Copyright © 1981, Ralph Pape

All Rights Reserved

SPECIAL NOTE

SPECIAL NOTE ON SONGS AND RECORDINGS

The title-play of this collection
is dedicated to:

Pete Sherayko

CONTENTS

GIRLS WE HAVE KNOWN

GIRLS WE HAVE KNOWN was first presented (in slightly different form) as a staged reading at Playwrights Horizons in December, 1981. The part of Alan was performed by Mark Blum; the part of Ernie by Ben Masters.

The action of the play takes place in 1980, several days after the death of Henry Miller on June 9th.

The play should be staged leaving as much as possible to the audience's imagination. The mock-up of the truck need not be at all elaborate.

CHARACTERS

Alan
Ernie

GIRLS WE HAVE KNOWN

Kansas. 2 a.m. The front seat of a small truck. From a cassette player set in dashboard, we can hear a popular country song like "If I Said You Had A Beautiful Body, Would You Hold It Against Me?"*

Ernie is driving. He is tall and husky, wears cowboy hat, neckerchief, jeans, boots and flannel shirt; and drinks Margaritas out of a battered tin cup. He usually keeps one foot propped up against the panel (or hangs it out the window). If the actor playing Ernie smokes, he should smoke only blunt cigars (or cigarillos).

Across from Ernie sits Alan. Alan is slight of build, medium to tall, wears a stylish narrow-collar sport shirt, light cardigan slacks and loafers, and drinks an expensive Scotch which he pours 2 fingers at a time into a small plastic cup. He wears very handsome sunglasses. If the actor playing Alan smokes, he should smoke only cigarettes.

Both men are in their late 20's.

Alan turns down sound on the cassette player, and leans out his window, yawning.

ALAN. *(Reading from sign.)* "You are now entering Montezuma,

*See special note on copyright page.

7

Kansas." *(He sits back. Ernie waits a moment before turning the volume back up. Seconds pass. Alan again leans out the window, turning down the volume as he does so. Reads from sign.)* "You are now leaving Montezuma, Kansas." *(He sits back. Immediately, Ernie turns music back up, even louder than before. Alan watches him, then shuts cassette player off.)*

ERNIE. Hey, leave that on.

ALAN. Ernie, just because we're driving cross-country, do we have to be subjected to country music throughout the entire trip?

ERNIE. You didn't complain on the way *out* to L.A.

ALAN. I was being tactful. After all, it *is* your van.

ERNIE. I told you: this is a truck, not a van! Jesus Christ, Alan, don't you know the difference yet between a truck and a van? *(He turns cassette player back on; Alan immediately turns it off.)* Hey!

ALAN. Do you mind? It's putting me to sleep!

ERNIE. Well, that's *your* problem! *(He turns it back on; Alan turns it off.)*

ALAN. Look, you said you wanted to make another 100 miles before we set up camp, and if I fall asleep, there's no one to wake *you* if you fall asleep, and if you fall asleep, the van goes off the road—

ERNIE. Truck!

ALAN. —the truck goes off the road and crashes into a silo and we die. We die in fucking Kansas. Old men carrying pitchforks and chewing on blades of grass will stumble over our mutilated bodies in the dawn's early light on their way to milk the cows — do you understand what I'm trying to say, Ernie? I do not wish to die in Kansas. I don't want to even consider the possibility of dying in Kansas. I want to die back in New York City. In approximately the fourth decade of the 21st century.... or later, if possible.

ERNIE. 6 weeks and he can't wait to be back in New York. I don't get it.

8

ALAN. 6 weeks and you're talking about leaving New York and settling in L.A. I don't believe it.

ERNIE. California's where I belong, Alan. I knew it the minute we got out there. It's got everything I want.

ALAN. Horses and beautiful girls, not necessarily in that order. *(Ernie lifts off his hat and lets go with a big cowboy whoop.)*

ERNIE. YAAAAAH-HAAAA!

ALAN. Must you keep doing that?

ERNIE. *(Putting hat back on.)* Just trying to keep you awake, pardner. *(Ernie downs what's left of his drink and holds out the empty cup to Alan.)* I'm ready for another Margarita. *(Alan reaches down for a plastic pitcher; swirls contents around.)*

ALAN. Personally, I hope this cowboy image of yours is just a temporary aberration. *(He pours remaining contents into Ernie's cup, emptying the pitcher while barely filling the cup.)*

ERNIE. A temporary 'what?'

ALAN. To thine own self be true, Ernie.

ERNIE. This is me, man.

ALAN. Just because you learned how to ride a horse and you look halfway decent in a cowboy hat—

ERNIE. Look at Clint Eastwood in *Bronco Billy*. He was a shoe salesman back East before he put together his Wild West show and became the man he was meant to be.

ALAN. I should never have taken you to see that picture. *(Holds up bottle.)* Want some Scotch?

ERNIE. That's a writer's drink.

ALAN. *(Pouring for himself.)* No. Allow me to correct you. It is merely a sensible drink.

ERNIE. Ever since you sold that screenplay, all you drink is Scotch. And you can take off your sunglasses, the sun set 8 hours ago.

ALAN. *(Removing glasses and looking around.)* So it has. *(Beat.)* You know, in the excitement of driving out to Hollywood for the first time, I overlooked the fact that we'd also have to drive back.

ERNIE. Bored?

ALAN. Don't be ridiculous. How could anyone be bored driving through Kansas at 2 o'clock in the morning?

ERNIE. Well, if you weren't afraid to fly—

ALAN. *(Defensively.)* I'm not afraid to fly.

ERNIE. You're too cautious. You have to get out there and try things while you're young. That was the whole message of *Bronco Billy.*

ALAN. I've always thought of flight as a metaphor for the human spirit. I've never gotten used to the idea of people actually flying. I mean ... it's so literal.

ERNIE. Sure. You had a chance to ride the mechanical bull when we stopped over at Gilley's Place; you passed that up, too. You're just too cautious, that's all there is to it. *(Beat.)* I'm very disappointed in you, Alan. *(Beat.)* Very, very disappoint—

ALAN. Did you know that Henry Miller died?

ERNIE. *(To himself.)* He never listens to me!

ALAN. He died the night before we left L.A. *(Waits for a response.)* I said he died the night before we—

ERNIE. Yeah. So?

ALAN. Nothing. He was my favorite writer, that's all.

ERNIE. Henry Miller. Wasn't he the guy who was really into sex?

ALAN. That's a popular misconception.

ERNIE. Oh yeah? That's not what I heard. I heard that when he wasn't busy fucking all these women, he was writing books about it.

ALAN. He was an extraordinary man, Ernie. *(Beat.)* Spiritually *and* physically. *(Beat.)* And apparently, he was indefatigable. *(To Ernie, helpfully.)* That means he could always get it up.

ERNIE. Thank you.

ALAN. What people don't know, of course, is that he also suffered terribly through many unrequited love affairs. *(To Ernie.)* That means—

ERNIE. I wasn't born in a cave, Alan.

10

ALAN. Even in his 80's, he was still dreaming of a girl he loved in high school. He used to walk a mile out of his way, past her house, hoping just to catch a glimpse of her through the window. *(Beat.)* Henry was O.K. *(Pause.)*

ERNIE. You remember Kathleen Doyle? *(Looks at Alan; no reaction.)* You remember. 4th grade? Sister Eugene?

ALAN. *(Getting it suddenly.)* Oh, right. Of course.

ERNIE. Remember her?

ALAN. God. That huge red honker, the mustache, those big black hairs curling out of her—

ERNIE. Not Sister Eugene, Kathleen Doyle.

ALAN. *(Sleepy.)* Oh. Sorry.

ERNIE. Wake up! We've got a lot of miles to go.

ALAN. I'm up, I'm up.

ERNIE. I remember she was really cute. *(Pause.)*

ALAN. I remember she transferred into our school for just that one year. She used to stand by herself before the first bell, holding one hand behind her back, afraid to look anyone in the eye.

ERNIE. There was something about her hair.

ALAN. *(Thinking.)* She had long brown hair, and she always wore a flower in it.

ERNIE. O.K.

ALAN. And she always ate alone. *(Beat.)* Once at Friday mass, Sister Victoria slapped her because she was daydreaming during the Confetior. Her face turned bright red and the flower fell out of her hair.

ERNIE. Fucking Victoria, man. She wouldn't be afraid of that mechanical bull.

ALAN. She wouldn't be afraid if a nuclear warhead was heading right toward her. She'd just hold out her crucifix and command it to stop.

ERNIE. Mean lady.

ALAN. I only saw her smile once.

ERNIE. Sister Victoria never—

11

ALAN. Kathleen Doyle, I mean. She was always reading these books, you know, these library books. Great reader. Sitting by herself on that big rock at lunchtime. So one day she looked up and saw me watching her and she smiled. I just froze.

ERNIE. Oh yeah?

ALAN. Could not utter a sound. Could not get the tongue to work. She just kept smiling. Apparently, she was fascinated because my fudgesickle was dripping down the front of my shirt and I didn't seem to know it. *(Beat.)* God.

ERNIE. I just remember she was really cute.

ALAN. I felt like Charlie Brown.

ERNIE. You looked like Charlie Brown.

ALAN. I admit I was awkward, but at least I wasn't fat.

ERNIE. Had to bring that up, didn't you?

ALAN. What are friends for?

ERNIE. I asked Judy Turner to dance with me in 7th grade and she said no because I was too fat.

ALAN. Girls are wonderful, aren't they?

ERNIE. Can you imagine how I felt?

ALAN. Too bad Judy Turner couldn't see you now. She'd eat her heart out.

ERNIE. I wouldn't buy Judy Turner a fucking cup of coffee.

ALAN. That's the spirit: forgive and forget.

ERNIE. I HATED GRAMMAR SCHOOL!

ALAN. Ernie, everyone hated grammar school.

ERNIE. I hated it more.

ALAN. I guess I shouldn't tell you this, but.

ERNIE. Tell me what?

ALAN. Judy Turner was the first girl I ever made out with. *(Beat.)*

ERNIE. *(Quite serious.)* When did this take place?

ALAN. Oh, it was so long ago.

ERNIE. Make an effort.

ALAN. 8th grade. Old man Lang's movie house. Sunday matinee. *I Was A Teenage Werewolf.*

12

ERNIE. I knew she had a crush on you—

ALAN. Yes. I knew you knew.

ERNIE. Did you know I hated you?

ALAN. You hated me because she had a crush on me?

ERNIE. Those nights we played Monopoly? You know what I really wanted to do? I wanted to take all those little houses and hotels and I wanted to shove them down your throat. And there were times when we'd be playing Chinese Checkers and all I could think of was wanting to grab a handful of those fucking marbles and just— *(Beat.)* Why didn't you tell me back then that you were having a thing with her?

ALAN. Believe it or not, I had this crazy idea you might not take it well.

ERNIE. Look, from now on, I don't want you to be afraid to tell me things.

ALAN. Yes, sir.

ERNIE. I'm serious. *(Beat.)* So? Did you think she was beautiful? Judy Turner?

ALAN. Kathleen Doyle was beautiful. Judy Turner was cute.

ERNIE. Come on. Kathleen Doyle was cute, but she wasn't beautiful. Judy Turner was beautiful.

ALAN. I beg to differ.

ERNIE. How come you're always the one who's right and I'm always the one who's wrong?

ALAN. Judy Turner was only beautiful in your mind. You put her on a pedestal because you knew you couldn't have her. That's classic.

ERNIE. Now wait a minute.

ALAN. If she had condescended to dance with you — taking into consideration the low esteem in which you held yourself at that time — you would have seen her in a much more realistic light.

ERNIE. Do you enjoy insulting me? Or is it just like a reflex with you?

ALAN. I'm not insulting you. *(Thinks.)* Wait a minute. I *am*

13

insulting you.

ERNIE. Just because I make my living hanging out in poolhalls doesn't mean I don't have feelings.

ALAN. You're right. I apologize. *(Pause.)*

ERNIE. *(Decisively.)* I say she was beautiful. *(He takes out a Colt 45 from beneath the seat and points it at Alan.)* Any objections?

ALAN. You would've been great on the high school debating team. *(Ernie holds gun aloft, pulls trigger; all we hear is a click.)*

ERNIE. YAAAA-HAAAA!

ALAN. You shot your rattlesnake in Flagstaff. Is it still necessary to keep that up here?

ERNIE. It's not loaded.

ALAN. I know it's not loaded. Could we please change the subject?

ERNIE. Shoot. *(Alan reacts to this.)* Sorry. *(He puts the gun away.)*

ALAN. Were you ever in love?

ERNIE. I don't think about it.

ALAN. That's not an answer.

ERNIE. Were *you* ever in love?

ALAN. I asked you first.

ERNIE. *(Mimicking.)* "I asked you first." *(Beat.)* I told you: I don't think about it.

ALAN. Ernie, your refusal to confront certain things about yourself is fascinating.

ERNIE. I don't see it that way.

ALAN. Oh, I know. That's why I'm giving you my evaluation as an objective observer.

ERNIE. You can't be an objective observer. We've known each other too long.

ALAN. Yes, but I'm capable of distancing myself from that.

ERNIE. Why is it any of your business if I've ever been in love?

ALAN. I'm a writer. I collect facts. A fact is a very beautiful thing. My chiropracter said that.

14

ERNIE. Speaking of facts, where the hell are we?

ALAN. Kansas.

ERNIE. I know that. Where in Kansas?

ALAN. About 20 minutes outside Montezuma.

ERNIE. I know that — what comes next?

ALAN. What town?

ERNIE. Yes, what town. Wake up.

ALAN. I have no idea.

ERNIE. Look in the glove compartment for the map.

ALAN. Oh, fuck it. Let's just drive.

ERNIE. I thought you collected facts.

ALAN. Certain kinds of facts.

ERNIE. Ah. Certain kinds of facts.

ALAN. That's right.

ERNIE. But not facts like where we are or how to clean and oil a gun or the difference between a truck and a van or how to change the fan-belt.

ALAN. I'm not a mechanic.

ERNIE. What would you have done if you were driving cross-country by yourself and had to change the fan-belt?

ALAN. Fortunately, we were together when the fan-belt broke.

ERNIE. Yeah, fortunately. Did you watch me when I was fixing it? So that you could do it if you had to? Nooooo.

ALAN. That's book knowledge. You can look that up in a book. Like the capital of a state or which country exports tin.

ERNIE. Or where we are.

ALAN. Right. You can always look that up on a map.

ERNIE. THAT'S WHAT I'M ASKING YOU TO DO!

ALAN. Why are you so obsessed about where we are?

ERNIE. For the same reason I like to know how to change a fan-belt or when a girl's having her period. Because it comes in handy to know these things. Don't you want to know where we are?

ALAN. It's more romantic this way. Who knows? We may turn a bend in the road and see 2 girls hitch-hiking. The girls we've

been waiting all our lives to meet. They're in danger. Someone's following them. We give them a lift and they—

ERNIE. Do you see a bend in this road?

ALAN. *(Stretching to look.)* No.

ERNIE. *Have* you seen a bend in this road?

ALAN. Not exactly.

ERNIE. Because this road is a straightaway, Alan. It goes on
like this without a break for 50 miles at a stretch. Because that's
what roads are like in Kansas. You won't find the girl of your
dreams around the next bend, because there is no next bend.
You'll be lucky to find another car. Do you realize we haven't
passed another car in over an hour?

ALAN. *(Quietly.)* My God, that's right. *(He looks around.)* That's
very strange, isn't it?

ERNIE. Do you want my honest opinion of what's wrong
with you?

ALAN. No, I do not.

ERNIE. You read too much.

ALAN. He tells me anyway.

ERNIE. You should stop reading for a while. A couple of years,
say. Do things, don't read about them. Pretend you're like Ben
Gazarra in *Run For Your Life*. You've got a rare disease, you're
doomed, you're going to die, there's nothing holding you back
anymore—

ALAN. Root Beer Barrels! *(Ernie just looks at him.)* That's what I
was trying to remember! When I was kissing Judy Turner in the
movies, she'd been eating Root Beer Barrels. *(To himself.)* Sweet-
est kiss I ever had. *(To Ernie.)* You remember those little candies,
don't you? Those Root Beer Barrels? *(Ernie turns the wheel sharply; brakes; shuts off ignition.)* What's the matter? Why are you
stopping?

ERNIE. I want to explore those woods over there. Get out.

ALAN. I'll wait here, thank you.

ERNIE. Oh no, you're coming with me.

ALAN. I am not. *(Ernie takes out gun and points it at him.)*

16

ERNIE. Get out of the truck.

ALAN. Don't do that, huh? Don't point that gun at me, dammit. *(Ernie opens it and shows it to Alan.)*

ERNIE. You see any bullets in there?

ALAN. I don't care if it's empty. I told you I hate guns, I hate that shit. If you're crazy enough to want to go exploring, fine, but don't expect me to—

ERNIE. Alan?

ALAN. What?

ERNIE. Relax. *(Smiling, he puts away gun.)* I only stopped so I could mix up some more Margaritas.

ALAN. Oh. *(Relieved.)* Well, why didn't you say so?

ERNIE. *(Getting out of truck.)* Had you going there for a minute, eh, pardner?

ALAN. *(Getting out of truck.)* The John Wayne school of stand-up comedy: laugh or I'll blow your brains out. *(Ernie moves off to take a leak. Alan looks around, suddenly rears back and cups his hands to his mouth.)* HEL-LLLLLLLLLLOOOO.

ERNIE. What are you doing?

ALAN. Waiting for the echo.

ERNIE. You're going to have a hell of a long wait.

ALAN. Oh, that's right, you have to have mountains or something for the... *(Feeling foolish.)* ...for the echo to ... to bounce off ... or something...

ERNIE. Brilliant, Alan.

ALAN. It's probably a common mistake.

ERNIE. Never mind. This could be an all-time record-breaking piss, so go ahead and start mixing the drinks.

ALAN. I don't know how.

ERNIE. He doesn't know how.

ALAN. I don't drink Margaritas, Ernie. Why should I be expected to know how to—?

ERNIE. *(Cutting him off.)* Do you think you can get the ice out of the cooler and dump some into the pitcher?

ALAN. I believe I can manage that, yes. *(He gets the cooler from the*

17

"back" of the truck.) I want to ask you something.

ERNIE. Yeah? *(Alan starts dumping some ice into the pitcher.)*

ALAN. Do you ever get nervous when you meet a really beautiful girl?

ERNIE. Who? Me? *(Ernie finishes pissing, goes over to the truck.)* What's there to be nervous about?

ALAN. It's never happened to you? *(Ernie gets the ingredients from the truck: Triple Sec, Tequila, lemon juice and salt.)*

ERNIE. Once — maybe.

ALAN. You felt ... vulnerable, right?

ERNIE. Well, if I did, I sure as hell didn't let *her* know it.

ALAN. Yes, but vulnerability in a man is a quality many women are supposed to find attractive.

ERNIE. Where do you get these ideas, Alan?!

ALAN. Well, in *Playboy*, they've been conducting these interviews with former playmates—

ERNIE. I love this. Go ahead.

ALAN. —and they all say that it's unfortunate that the average guy is afraid to approach them because they're—

ERNIE. Don't tell me. Because they're so gorgeous?

ALAN. That's right.

ERNIE. When actually they're really lonely? Am I close?

ALAN. What they said was that it's precisely this shyness in a man, this vulnerability—

ERNIE. *(Laughing.)* Yeah? Yeah?

ALAN. —which would make them open up to him, if only he could believe in himself enough to—

ERNIE. Alan, what they mean is that if a guy looks like Burt Reynolds or Clint Eastwood — *and just happens to act a little shy* — you know, like maybe he trips getting out of his Rolls Royce with all these photographers around, and he laughs about it, and there's this chick standing there, and he lets her help him up, and he gives her this little smile and asks her if she'd like to come into Studio 54 with him — THEN, and only then, does the chick think: Hey, I think I like this guy, he's really vulnerable.

ALAN. That's not what they said in the—

ERNIE. Read between the lines, my friend. *(Beat.)* Do *you* get nervous when you meet a really beautiful girl?

ALAN. I assumed most men did. Apparently, I was wrong.

ERNIE. Alan, what is there to get nervous about?

ALAN. I don't know, it's just—

ERNIE. You have got to be the most nervous person I've ever met.

ALAN. I'd prefer to think of it as a by-product of my sensitivity. *(Beat.)* You really mean that?

ERNIE. Yes, I do.

ALAN. Really?

ERNIE. Look at how you acted last week.

ALAN. How did I act?

ERNIE. We're eating dinner. Then this debate comes on the TV about the MX missile. You get white as a ghost. Your hand starts shaking. You drop your fork. Then you excuse yourself and go outside. Letting a terrific meal go to waste. Which by the way I spent 2 hours slaving over in a hot kitchen because you never learned how to cook anything that's not frozen, but that's beside the point.

ALAN. Oh. That.

ERNIE. Yeah. That.

ALAN. You're right. I can't lay the blame for *all* my insecurities on the age in which we happen to be living.

ERNIE. I'm glad to hear you say that.

ALAN. I mean .. I realize that each one of us has to accept sole responsibility for who he is. *(Beat.)* Even me. *(Beat.)* Although, to be honest, I've often felt an exception should be made in my case.

ERNIE. Well, it's not, so just forget it. Now. Getting back to the beautiful girls. I don't see what your problem is.

ALAN. You don't?

ERNIE. Let's look at the facts. You've lived with some pretty decent chicks, right? What about Karen? And that waitress who played the flute?

ALAN. Oboe.

ERNIE. Was that her name?

ALAN. Her name was Adrien. She played the oboe.

ERNIE. Adrien, right. She wasn't bad. Talked too much, but—

ALAN. Ernie, what I'm referring to is that existential moment when you see a girl for the first time, and you're deeply attracted to her, and you know that unless you act fast, you're never going to meet her. You're going to lose that chance forever. Understand? *(Ernie seems to be contemplating this.)* Well?

ERNIE. Aren't you going to tell me what "existential" means?

ALAN. *(Ignoring this.)* On 3 occasions, I took the initiative, walked over, introduced myself to a girl I had never met before and told her exactly what was on my mind.

ERNIE. Why you dirty little—

ALAN. Ernie. Please. *(Beat.)* One girl was walking across the street as I was getting out of a cab, another was waiting for a bus, the third was passing by me on the opposite escalator.

ERNIE. Don't tell me. You slid down the bannister and introduced yourself as you—

ALAN. I followed her out of the store!

ERNIE. O.K., O.K., don't get excited. So what did you say to these chicks?

ALAN. Well ... first I said: "Excuse me?"

ERNIE. Brilliant.

ALAN. I said: "Excuse me, you don't know who I am, but when I saw you just now, I knew I had to meet you." *(Ernie is finishing his first drink. Alan waits.)*

ERNIE. I'm listening. *(Ernie moves around the area, looking around, stretching and not paying Alan much attention.)*

ALAN. "I was afraid if I didn't tell you this now, I'd never see you again. I'd never get this chance again. I know it sounds crazy, but I really had to meet you."

ERNIE. You're making this up.

ALAN. I swear to God.

ERNIE. So? Did you get laid?

ALAN. Must you be so crude?

ERNIE. Did you get laid?

ALAN. 2 out of 3.

ERNIE. 2 out of 3 ain't bad. How'd that line go again?

ALAN. It wasn't a line! That's just it. I really meant what I said.

ERNIE. *(Incredulous.)* You meant it?

ALAN. I never know when it's going to happen. It just comes over me. I have to feel it, otherwise it's no good.

ERNIE. Let me see if I understand this: you have to *feel* it?

ALAN. I have to feel it.

ERNIE. My boy, you have a serious problem.

ALAN. Thanks. *(Ernie looks around some more.)*

ERNIE. Hey. I'm tired. Why don't we just set up camp here?

ALAN. We're in the middle of nowhere.

ERNIE. Look: full moon. Stars. What more do you want?

ALAN. People.

ERNIE. Quit complaining, huh? Give me a hand. *(Ernie starts to pull out the sleeping bags from the back of the truck. Also some firewood which they have previously collected. Alan helps him, reluctantly.)*

ALAN. I thought we agreed to always set up camp in an authorized rest area.

ERNIE. Hold this, will you? *(Ernie hands Alan his drink, as he begins to untie the sleeping bags.)*

ALAN. Ernie?

ERNIE. Speak to me, Alan.

ALAN. I suppose you have a standard line you use all the time, right? When you see a girl in a bar, for example? *(Ernie just grins at him.)* You bastard. What's your opening line?

ERNIE. Well, I'll tell you.... *(Beat.)* I usually wait for the girl to make the first move.

ALAN. Oh, well, pardon me.

ERNIE. Don't knock it if you haven't tried it. It works.

ALAN. *(Skeptical.)* It does, huh?

ERNIE. It gives you this air of mystery. *(He takes back his cup and gives us his profile.)* You never say a word to anybody, see? You just stand like this, sipping your drink, looking up at the ceiling. *(Beat.)*

ALAN. What happens if the girl never makes the first move? *(Beat.)* What happens if the girl never makes the first move?

ERNIE. You feel very dumb. *(They both smile. Ernie holds out his cup, offering Alan a drink. Alan takes the cup and studies it.)*

ALAN. If I started drinking these regularly, would I become like you?

ERNIE. If you're lucky. *(Alan drinks, makes a face and hands it back. Ernie starts building the fire, piling up the wood expertly. At no time does the fire ever get lit.)*

ALAN. *(Looking around.)* Spooky out here.

ERNIE. Hey. How many girls you been to bed with?

ALAN. I'm sorry, Ernie, I left my pocket calculator back in New York. *(Standing.)* Listen, I've been giving this some serious thought, and I really think we should keep driving like we originally planned. You know? Ernie?

ERNIE. You remember that blonde I brought back to the apartment the first week in L.A.? 19 years old? The one with the slit evening dress and the jewelry?

ALAN. The one you picked up at Barney's Beanery?

ERNIE. Yeah. What the hell was her name again?

ALAN. Phyllis.

ERNIE. That's it: Phyllis. You know what she said to me? You're not going to believe this.

ALAN. What?

ERNIE. She said by the time she was 14 — 14! — she'd gone to bed with over 50 different guys! What do you think of that?

ALAN. Nice round number.

ERNIE. Can you believe that?

ALAN. We have to face facts, Ernie. These kids of today just don't have the hang-ups about sex that we did when we were—

ERNIE. HEY! We're talking about 50 guys, here!

ALAN. Yes, I know.

ERNIE. That's a lot of guys, Alan!

ALAN. She tell you about this in bed?

ERNIE. Yeah. She was one of those goddamn talkers. I hate that.

ALAN. Hearing about all those guys didn't—?

ERNIE. Didn't what?

ALAN. Interfere with your, you know, performance?

ERNIE. She told me about the 50 guys after we'd already ... performed. *(Beat.)* This is just between us, O.K.?

ALAN. O.K.

ERNIE. I think she was a little disappointed in me.

ALAN. Really?

ERNIE. I know. I can't believe it either.

ALAN. She was insatiable, was she?

ERNIE. *(Confused.)* Yeah ... yeah.

ALAN. *(Helpfully.)* "Incapable of being satisfied."

ERNIE. I know what the hell it means! *(Beat.)* Really wore me out. Phew! *(To himself.)* 50 guys! I just can't get over that. What the fuck number was I, I wonder.

ALAN. I would say this experience had a profound effect upon you.

ERNIE. Well, hey, I figured I'd been around, you know, but Jesus Christ.

ALAN. Look at it this way: maybe she's just ... incredibly healthy, sexually.

ERNIE. She's fucked-up is what she is. You want a drink?

ALAN. I want to leave!

ERNIE. 50 guys, Alan!

ALAN. Well, *you've* slept around.

ERNIE. Yeah, but I'm not—

ALAN. Insatiable?

23

ERNIE. Damn right. Even when I was stationed in North Carolina and I was screwing these 3 sisters — O.K., I admit it, I put in a lot of serious fucking when I was down South, but I didn't go crazy or anything. Not like what's-her-name.

ALAN. Excuse me. You were sleeping with 3 members of the same family?

ERNIE. April. May. And June.

ALAN. You're full of shit.

ERNIE. Hey, I shouldn't even be telling you this. This is *personal.* The point is—

ALAN. The point is you're full of shit.

ERNIE. I was 19. Never been to bed with a girl — hard to believe, I know. And these 3 sisters were living in a complex near the Air Force Base. Out of their minds, these girls. Had a thing for servicemen. April was the very first girl I went to bed with, May was the second, June was the third. All in the same week. Man, those girls kept me busy *that* summer.

ALAN. Excuse me. Are you telling me that this arrangement lasted an entire summer?

ERNIE. Isn't this an incredible story?

ALAN. Yeah, but how did you—?

ERNIE. Here's how it worked. April didn't know I was fucking June. And June didn't know I was fucking April — but she suspected me of fucking May. Now April knew I was fucking May, but she didn't care, because I told her that May meant nothing to me, and I was going to break it off the next time I saw her.

ALAN. What about May?

ERNIE. She thought we were getting married.

ALAN. How did she get that idea?

ERNIE. I told her we were.

ALAN. I see.

ERNIE. So she was making wedding plans, and meanwhile I'm still fucking April and June.

ALAN. You sure you never read Henry Miller?

24

ERNIE. Don't get me sidetracked, Alan. The point is: this is not a story I'd go around telling to people. Look, I never even told it to you. And I sure as hell wouldn't blurt it out to some chick I'm in the sack with.

ALAN. And with good reason.

ERNIE. No, no, you don't understand — because it's *personal*, man. Hey, there's a lot of things you don't know about me. There's a *lot* of things I choose to keep to myself, all right? Now why do you suppose, Alan, that I choose to keep my feelings to myself? Have you ever asked yourself that?

ALAN. I assumed it had something to do with your hero-worship of Clint Eastwood.

ERNIE. I don't *worship* Clint Eastwood: I fucking *admire* the man, that's all. Because he doesn't waste words.

ALAN. No, he certainly doesn't.

ERNIE. Because he has enough sense to keep his feelings to himself. And you know why? Because he knows it serves no purpose, Alan. Trying to explain your feelings to somebody else serves no fucking purpose whatsoever, except to drive the other person nuts. Now, I'm not saying that that's what you've done to me—

ALAN. How did I get into this?

ERNIE. Alan, look, we go back a long way, you and me. And it's funny, you know, the two of us don't have that much in common, but for some weird fucking reason — which there is no need to put into *words*, O.K.? — we've remained friends. Even when we lose touch, we know the other guy will always be there if one of us is in a jam and needs help. Like when you needed to come out to L.A., but you were afraid to fly—

ALAN. I'm not afraid to fly—

ERNIE. —I was there, O.K.? I was there with my wheels to help my buddy out — and don't get me wrong, I was happy to do it. But let's be honest: it hasn't been easy cooped up with you in the front of this truck day in and day out, I mean, if I didn't have a tape deck, Jesus — but the *point*, Alan, what I was trying

25

to say before you got me sidetracked is that even you, at your worst, aren't as bad as that goddamn Phyllis. I mean it's bad enough she tells me about the 50 guys, which she should've had the decency to keep to herself, O.K.? But then she tells me about her kid who's staying with her sick mother in Houston, then she tells me about her younger sister who committed suicide because she couldn't *cope* or something, then she tells me about her husband who just up and disappeared 6 months ago — and she couldn't figure out why! That's the part that killed me! *Then* she goes on for about 15 minutes about how the situation in the Middle East has really got her depressed —you get the picture? So I said: look. Phyllis. I don't talk, understand? You got problems, I got problems, Johnny Carson's got problems, everybody's got problems. Let's leave our problems outside the bedroom like civilized people. *(Beat.)*

ALAN. She told me you said that. She seemed a little hurt.

ERNIE. When was *this?*

ALAN. I'll just put the sleeping bags in the back and then we can—

ERNIE. Don't touch anything, Alan. Now, when exactly was this?

ALAN. She came back the next night, looking for you. You were at the Palamino Club, trying to track down that barmaid you—

ERNIE. That part I know.

ALAN. I offered her a drink. We talked.

ERNIE. About me?

ALAN. About a lot of things. She's really very intelligent.

ERNIE. Yeah. Sure.

ALAN. She speaks 3 languages. She's working for her degree in—

ERNIE. I'm not interested. O.K.? I'm not interested.

ALAN. We watched a National Geographic Special together.

ERNIE. I'm not interested.

ALAN. Can we go now? Please?

ERNIE. Who said anything about going?

ALAN. Thanks a lot.

ERNIE. Relax. Have a drink. I'll match you. Two to your one.

ALAN. We also went to bed. *(Beat.)* I wasn't going to tell you.

ERNIE. I love this. I find the girl, he fucks her.

ALAN. You told me not to be afraid to tell you anything.

ERNIE. When did I say that?

ALAN. About 20 minutes ago.

ERNIE. *(Trying to remember.)* Well, if I said it, then I meant it.

ALAN. She really liked you.

ERNIE. Wait a minute. Did she tell you about the 50 guys?

ALAN. Yes, she did.

ERNIE. Well, why the hell didn't you stop me if you heard all this already?

ALAN. You seemed to have this real need to talk about it, so—

ERNIE. What need? I don't have any needs!

ALAN. I'm not trying to pass judgment on you.

ERNIE. What else did she say? About me?

ALAN. Oh, about you getting tired and all.

ERNIE. Listen, you'd get tired too if you tried to satisfy a girl who fucked a hundred guys before she turned fourteen!

ALAN. 50 guys.

ERNIE. What are you doing? Sticking up for her?

ALAN. I didn't get tired.

ERNIE. *(Mimicking.)* "I didn't get tired."

ALAN. Ernie, seriously, let's go, O.K.? I'll drive if you're too … fatigued.

ERNIE. Not so fast, pardner. Not so fast. *(Ernie is standing. He surveys the surroundings.)* I'll bet you whatever you want you haven't got the balls to explore those woods.

ALAN. You're an excellent judge of character. May we leave now?

ERNIE. You really want to leave?

ALAN. Desperately.

ERNIE. O.K. I'll make you a deal. You explore those woods by yourself, and then we'll leave. How's that?

ALAN. Forget it!

ERNIE. O.K. You don't explore those woods, we stay right here.

ALAN. Who do I look like? Davy Crockett?

ERNIE. Scared?

ALAN. No. It's just so dumb, that's all.

ERNIE. O.K. You say you're not scared. Then tell me one thing you've done in the last year that took real courage.

ALAN. I took a ride on the IRT.

ERNIE. Good. That's a good beginning. This is the next step.

ALAN. You want me to tell you why you're really doing this? This is your way of getting back at me because I went to bed with ... with—

ERNIE. What's this? You can't remember?

ALAN. I'm the one who told you her name before!

ERNIE. Pretty good, you go to bed with an intelligent, sensitive human being, you get your rocks off, you forget her name. Very nice.

ALAN. Phyllis!

ERNIE. Phyllis, right. Well, you're wrong, that's not the reason. I'm doing this for your own good, Alan, and that's the truth.

ALAN. Look, I went to bed with a girl you picked up, you want me to apologize for that, fine, I'll apologize.

ERNIE. Don't apologize. I would've done the same thing myself.

ALAN. Jesus, you'd think this was the first time I went to bed with a girl you picked up.

ERNIE. This has happened before?

ALAN. Why am I telling him this?

ERNIE. How long has this been going on, Alan?

ALAN. It's not important. Can we please go now?

ERNIE. Sounds like you should be paying me a commission.

ALAN. Ernie, it's your own fault! If you would only talk to these girls besides fucking them, they wouldn't have to go elsewhere for a little conversation.

ERNIE. I don't mind the conversation part.

ALAN. You have no right to be angry with me and you know that.

ERNIE. I'm not angry. Look. I'm smiling.

ALAN. You're drunk.

ERNIE. Why don't you want to go in the woods?

ALAN. Because.

ERNIE. Think how much confidence you'll have in yourself after you do this. Just stop and think.

ALAN. *(Looking.)* It's dark in there.

ERNIE. Don't move. *(He races to the truck, gets the gun and puts it in Alan's hand. Also, a tiny pocket flashlight.)* Make me proud of you. *(Alan takes a few tentative steps toward the woods.)*

ALAN. I must be crazy. I don't know why I'm doing this.

ERNIE. Because deep down you know I'm right. You have to deal with your fears, that's all there is to it. *(Alan takes one step into the woods.)* 'Atta boy. *(Alan stops.)* You stopped. Why are you stopping? Don't stop.

ALAN. I'm checking it out, do you mind? *(He walks along the edge of the audience, peering into the "woods.")*

ERNIE. Look, pretend you're out camping with this chick — gorgeous chick, O.K.? The kind you're afraid to walk up to.

ALAN. Will you shut up? I'm trying to concentrate.

ERNIE. *(Acting out both parts.)* She hears a noise. She's scared. She puts her arms around you, practically suffocating you with her tits. *(As the girl.)* "Oh Alan, what are we going to do?" *(As himself.)* You take her by the shoulders and shake her. *(As Alan.)* "HEY, COOL IT!"

ALAN. *(Still peering into woods.)* The psychological approach.

ERNIE. *(As Alan.)* "As long as I'm here to protect you, you don't have to worry about what's out there in those woods, I can take care of it, understand?" *(Beat.)* "Hey, I'm talking to you!"

ALAN. *(Turning; confused.)* To me?

ERNIE. No! To the chick.

ALAN. Pardon me for interrupting myself.

ERNIE. *(As the girl.* "Yes, Alan. Yes, I understand." *(As Alan.)* "Good. Now get back under the fucking covers and don't make a sound." *(To Alan.)* See, now you have to go through with it. You've just made a complete asshole of yourself bragging to this chick, and if you don't go in the woods, you're really going to look like shit.

ALAN. Why can't I have normal friends like other people?

ERNIE. Alan, the time is now. The choice is yours.

ALAN. *(Entering the woods.)* I feel like a fool.

ERNIE. You look great.

ALAN. Wait a minute, this gun isn't even loaded.

ERNIE. Well, of course not. I know how you feel about guns.

ALAN. Ernie!

ERNIE. Someday you'll thank me for this.

ALAN. *(Stopping.)* Shit.

ERNIE. What?

ALAN. Over there.

ERNIE. I don't see anything.

ALAN. Get in here. I'll show you.

ERNIE. You just want company. *(Ernie enters and looks around.)* Well?

ALAN. Over there.

ERNIE. *(Looking.)* That's a tree.

ALAN. I know it's a tree. Intellectually, I know it's a tree.

ERNIE. So? *(Pause. Alan fidgets.)* So?!

ALAN. *(Embarrassed to say it.)* It looks like Rod Serling. *(Ernie looks at Alan, then at the tree, then back at Alan.)*

ERNIE. That's a tree!

ALAN. Yes, I know. *(Beat.)* See how it looks like he's holding his hands clasped in front of him?

ERNIE. Those are branches!

ALAN. I know that. *(Beat.)* I tried to tell you this wasn't going to work.

ERNIE. *(Mock-serious Western drawl.)* Son, I knowed how much he meant to you, but old Rod's in the Twilight Zone now, rest his soul, and he ain't never gonna be comin' back this way again. Not even as a tree. *(Alan starts to walk past Ernie, out of the woods. Ernie drops accent.)* Where do you think you're going? *(He runs ahead, blocking Alan's path.)* Don't tell me you're giving up?

ALAN. Are you going to get out of my way?

ERNIE. Alan, you have to go back in there!

ALAN. Look, I don't want to explore any goddamn woods! And if I live to be a hundred, it really won't bother me if I've never had a ride on some fucking mechanical bull! Now kindly step aside.

ERNIE. This is for your own good!

ALAN. All right. I admit it. I'm a coward. All right? I admit it! Now what else do you want from me?

ERNIE. I want you to go in those woods! *(Without realizing it, Alan now starts to point the gun at Ernie's chest.)*

ALAN. Can't you get it through your head that I'm not interested in competing with anybody? Do you understand? Not with you, not with Clint Eastwood, not with—

ERNIE. Alan.

ALAN. *(Poking him with the gun.)* Do. You. Under. Stand?

ERNIE. Alan.

ALAN. Shut up! If I'm going to compete with somebody, it's going to be with myself, all right? Is that clear?

ERNIE. Would you please take a look at what you're doing?

ALAN. Don't interrupt me! I'm not through!

ERNIE. *(Pointing.)* Look. *(Alan now sees he's been pointing the gun at Ernie.)*

31

ALAN. Jesus.

ERNIE. It's O.K. It's not loaded. *(He takes gun; opens it.)* See?

ALAN. I could've killed you.

ERNIE. *(Laughing.)* Not without any bullets.

ALAN. I was pointing a gun at you! I had my finger on the trigger!

ERNIE. It's O.K.

ALAN. It's not O.K.

ERNIE. Alan, relax. *(Alan starts picking up the blankets and the bottles and pieces of firewood and throwing them in the back of the truck.)*

ALAN. Let's go!

ERNIE. You're over-reacting. *(Alan climbs into the driver's seat.)*

ALAN. You coming or what?

ERNIE. You better let me drive.

ALAN. *(Turning key in ignition.)* Let's move it, huh! I haven't got all night! *(Ernie picks up his cup and pitcher of Margaritas.)*

ERNIE. Alan, I said I'll drive—

ALAN. Goddammit, get in the van!

ERNIE. Truck, truck!

ALAN. TRUCK! *(Ernie gets in. Alan turns the wheel sharply and pulls out. Ernie watches him. Alan is hunched over the wheel intensely.)*

ERNIE. You sure you don't want me to—?

ALAN. No! I don't want you saying I didn't do my share of the driving, now just shut up! *(Ernie drinks, watches Alan, the road, the speedometer.)*

ERNIE. You want to try to stay on the road?

ALAN. I'm on the road! *(Ernie looks out his window down at the road, then back at Alan.)*

ERNIE. All right. I'm not going to say anything. *(He sips his drink calmly. Alan is still hunched intensely over the wheel.* Be like that. See if I care. *(Pause. Ernie repeatedly glances at the speedometer.)* I guess you know how fast you're going. *(Pause.)* You do know you're going 90 miles an hour, don't you? *(Alan never glances at the speedometer.)* Alan? *(Beat.)* Alan! Look at the speedometer.

ALAN. I can't.

ERNIE. What do you mean you can't?

ALAN. I can't move!

ERNIE. This is no time to be joking, Alan. *(Beat. Ernie leans across to look into Alan's face.)* Alan?

ALAN. WHHHHOOAAAAOOOWWW!

ERNIE. Alan, don't panic. Sit back. Sit back and follow my instructions. Ease your foot off the gas. *(Beat.)* ALAN! *(Ernie grabs his window frame for support, as the motion buffets him from side to side.)* Stay on the fucking road!

ALAN. I'm trying! *(Ernie grabs hold of Alan, tries to pull his body back from the wheel.)*

ERNIE. Let your body relax.

ALAN. I'm trying!

ERNIE. *(Struggling with him.)* Alan. Listen. Repeat after me: I don't want to die in Kansas!

ALAN. I don't want to die in Kansas! I don't want to die in —

ERNIE. Good, good, come on back, that's it. *(He pulls Alan erect.)* Come on. O.K. Now. Can you lift your foot off the gas?

ALAN. I can't even feel my foot!

ERNIE. I'll help you. *(Ernie grabs hold of Alan's leg.)* I'm going to put your foot on the brake.

ALAN. O.K.

ERNIE. Your foot is now on the brake.

ALAN. O.K.

ERNIE. Now very gently press down on the— *(Alan brakes so suddenly that they are both hurled forward. Ernie braces himself against the dashboard. Slowly, they both sit back in their seats.*

ALAN. Have we stopped?

ERNIE. You could say that.

ALAN. I'm sorry. I'm truly sorry.

ERNIE. These things happen. *(Alan gets out of the truck and tries to stand. His legs are like rubber.)*

ALAN. Oh boy.

ERNIE. You O.K.?

ALAN. I don't know. *(Beat.)* I think I'm going to be sick. *(Beat.)* Maybe not. *(Beat.)* On the other hand. *(He leans against the truck, breathing deeply.)* Wow.

ERNIE. You want your Di-Gel tablets?

ALAN. Please. *(Ernie gets the Di-Gel tablets from the glove compartment, comes out and gives them to Alan. He starts to walk Alan around the playing area.)*

ERNIE. You know how fast you were going there, toward the end?

ALAN. Don't tell me.

ERNIE. You passed a hundred.

ALAN. He tells me anyway.

ERNIE. How you doing?

ALAN. Let me see if I can walk by myself. *(Ernie lets him go. Alan takes a few faltering steps.)*

ERNIE. 'Atta boy.

ALAN. I don't know what happened to me.

ERNIE. Keep walking. Breathe. *(Alan does this. As he walks back and forth, he appears to be reflecting on the situation.)*

ALAN. You know ... in a way ... it was ... kind of ... exhilirating.... *(He starts to walk with more assurance.)* I never experienced anything like that before. *(Beat.)* It was really exciting.

ERNIE. One way of putting it.

ALAN. Were you scared?

ERNIE. Hey, did I sound scared?

ALAN. You sounded terrified.

ERNIE. I was a little concerned.

ALAN. You were scared!

ERNIE. You're goddamn fucking right I was! *(They both start to laugh. Ernie gets Alan his Scotch, while he takes a big drink from his own pitcher.)*

ALAN. Whoo!

ERNIE. Damn *(They're having a great time.)*

ALAN. Ernie?

ERNIE. Speak to me, Alan.

ALAN. Up to a year ago, you'd never been on a horse, correct?

ERNIE. That is correct. Yes.

ALAN. So ... let's say ... if I really wanted to learn how to ride....?

ERNIE. You could do it, sure. Hell.

ALAN. If you really want to do something—

ERNIE. How do you think I dropped those 70 pounds?

ALAN. I have to give you credit for that.

ERNIE. You're no different than me. You just haven't wanted anything badly enough.

ALAN. I guess even if I wanted to do something really wild — let's say I wanted to sky-dive, for example.

ERNIE. Sky-dive?

ALAN. Not that I feel I have to prove anything to anybody, but if I really wanted to do it, I guess there's no reason why I couldn't. Sure. *(He walks about, savoring his confidence.)* Ernie, you know, this is incredible. I could do it. I could really fucking do it! ERNIE! WOW!

ERNIE. Alan, don't you have to get used to riding *in* an airplane first before you start jumping out of one?

ALAN. Oh.... Oh, that's right. I forgot about that. *(Ernie takes off his hat and plops it on Alan's head.)* What's this for? *(Ernie takes Alan's Scotch and has a long pull on it.)*

ERNIE. *(Meaning the hat.)* Those damn things give you a headache after a while. *(He sniffs the Scotch.)* Interesting. *(He holds out the Margarita pitcher to Alan. Alan takes a sip.)*

ALAN. Interesting. *(Alan holds out the pitcher, but Ernie gestures for him to keep it. They both drink.)* So. Did you ever think about getting married? *Really?*

ERNIE. Once. You?

ALAN. Twice.

ERNIE. So then, you're saying you were in love.

ALAN. Well ... so then ... must have ... been you. *(They both realize he's a little drunk.)*

ERNIE. Try to speak in sentences.

35

ALAN. Were you?

ERNIE. I asked you first.

ALAN. I used to fall in love all the time. I used to think it was love, anyway. Didn't take much, either. A smile, something about the eyes—

ERNIE. A flower in the hair?

ALAN. A flower in the hair, yeah. What the hell is that, anyway? That's not love. Although a lot of guys—

ERNIE. Richie Daly.

ALAN. Richie Daly. What did he always say about Marjorie? "I love her voice, I love her voice."

ERNIE. They're divorced.

ALAN. You can't fall in love with a voice. *(Pause.)* I've been seeing this woman for about six months. You've never met her or anything—

ERNIE. So?

ALAN. So I think maybe I'm in love with her.

ERNIE. You *think* you're in love with her? What's that supposed to mean?

ALAN. Boy, I don't know. You got me. I came across this old saying recently, to the effect that very few people would fall in love if they had never read about it. And I thought: God, that's so fucking depressing, it's probably true. But when I'm with this woman, Ernie, everything seems so *simple* and everything around us takes on such *clarity* that it seems beside the point whether you call it love or something else. And then I wonder if I'm worthy of it, of *her*, you know? That's the part that really scares me. *(Alan takes a drink and begins to recite, dramatizing unconsciously.)* "So whoever loves must try to act as if he had a great work: he must be much alone and go into himself and collect himself and hold fast to himself; he must work; he must become something!" Rilke said that. *(Beat.)*

ERNIE. Well, my friend, do you know what my advice to you is?

ALAN. What?

ERNIE. Don't think about it. *(Beat.)* Socrates said that.

ALAN. He did not.

ERNIE. Well. He meant to. *(Ernie goes off to take a leak, his back to the audience.)* If you can manage to stay under 100 miles an hour, I think I'll let you drive.

ALAN. I believe that can be arranged. *(Alan goes over and leans against the truck, looking up at the sky and still sipping from Ernie's pitcher.)*

ERNIE. Yeah, the only time I really thought about getting married was when I was going with Mary Crowley. Very sharp lady she was. *Very* sharp. She said, "Ernie, you know you're not ready for something like that." She was right. Of course, I didn't put up too much of an argument, either. But the funny thing was she kept in touch. For a while, anyway. Even after she got married and moved upstate. Her husband was a nice guy, too — although personally I thought she could've done better. But they loved each other, I'll say that for them. I used to pop in on 'em from time to time — give 'em some bullshit that there was a pool tournament nearby, and seeing as how I was in the neighborhood. We'd talk on the phone, too. She'd call me. I'd call her. Not a lot but. She'd want to know how I was doing. I'd lie. She'd catch me lying. Always knew. Very strange. She had a nice laugh, too. I'd call her and say, "So when are you going to leave your husband and run away with me?" She'd laugh. "Ernie, you know I'm a happily married woman." "Can't blame a guy for trying," I'd say. Just kidding around like that. Every Christmas, she sends me a picture of the family. *(Ernie finishes pissing and comes over to Alan.)* Yeah, I guess I should give her a call one of these days, see how she's doing. *(Alan turns to look at him, suddenly.)*

ALAN. You don't know?

ERNIE. Know what?

ALAN. Mary died last January. *(Beat.)*

ERNIE. She *died?*

ALAN. You were away for a couple of months. I guess I just

forgot about it. Figured you knew—

ERNIE. She *died?*

ALAN. I ran into George Zelasny and he showed me the clipping. You know his cousin is related to—

ERNIE. How did she die?

ALAN. She was alone. Coming back from grocery shopping. Her car was approaching this intersection when this truck ran a light. *(Pause.)*

ERNIE. Jesus.

ALAN. You O.K.?

ERNIE. Yeah, I'm just—

ALAN. *(Opening door.)* ... ready?

ERNIE. ... yeah, let's go. *(They both get into the truck with their drinks. Alan turns on the ignition and pulls out. Ernie takes out his wallet and shows Alan a snapshot.)* This was taken 2 Christmases ago.

ALAN. That her husband?

ERNIE. Yeah.

ALAN. Cute kids.

ERNIE. Yeah, they are, aren't they? And look. Do you believe this? Chickens. Goats. Goddamn *horses*, man.

ALAN. I love the way they're all standing around in front of that ... that ...

ERNIE. Tractor.

ALAN. *(Yawning.)* Tractor. I'm sorry. *(Alan studies the picture.)* You know what this reminds me of? The way they're standing? *(Alan hands back the picture. Ernie just keeps staring at it.)* Those photographic spreads you see in these arty magazines nowadays. You know which ones I mean? These young couples in their homes? Only instead of a farm behind them, there's like the skylight of their loft, maybe a piece of sculpture one of them's been working on, or an easel and paints, or ballet tights drying on a line. And they all have this same look, this great look. They stare right into the camera, like they're challenging it. They stare right back at you, very deliberately. Their arms around each other. *(Beat. Alan looks at Ernie, still staring at picture.)*

I'm sorry, man. I thought you knew.

ERNIE. Nope. I didn't. *(He puts picture away.)* Well, it's not like — shit, it's been years since I've even *seen* her, you know? It's not like—

ALAN. Yeah, I know what you mean. *(Beat.)* Want a little music?

ERNIE. Why not? *(Alan leans forward to turn on cassette player, but stops abruptly.)*

ALAN. Hey, do you think we're fucked up? Seriously.

ERNIE. What?

ALAN. I mean ... maybe that explains our friendship. Remember? You couldn't figure out why we — what we have in common?

ERNIE. But only one of us is fucked up, Alan, so how could that explain it?

(Smiling at Ernie, Alan turns on cassette player. Once again we hear a song like "If I Said You Had A Beautiful Body, Would You Hold It Against Me?"* Alan raises his drink to Ernie; Ernie smiles and raises his drink. They toast each other. Ernie turns away from Alan and stares out the window, lost in thought. Alan watches him for a moment, then settles in for a long ride, adjusting his cowboy hat, maybe even propping up his foot on the dashboard.)

FADE OUT

THE END

39

PROPERTY PLOT

Onstage

Front seat of a small truck with
   Steering wheel
   Dashboard, with cassette player
Tin cup
Plastic cup
Bottle of scotch
Bottle of triple sec
Bottle of tequila
Pitcher
Salt shaker
Lemon juice
2 sleeping bags
Firewood
Small pocket flashlight
Di-Gel tablets
45 Colt revolver
Cigarillos, cigarettes and matches (optional)
Ice cooler

Personal

Wallet (Ernie)
Snapshot (Ernie)

WARM AND TENDER LOVE

WARM AND TENDER LOVE was originally commissioned by Actors Theatre of Louisville in 1982.

Vinnie's singing is an attempt to mimic the unique style of Percy Sledge. The original version of the song, "Warm and Tender Love" can be heard on *The Best of Percy Sledge,* available on Atlantic records and tapes.*

The time of the play is the present.

CHARACTERS

Man (Vinnie)
Woman (Elena)

*See Special Note on Copyright Page.

WARM AND TENDER LOVE

Interior of a sauna in a small New York health club. It is empty except for a Young Man in his early 20's. He has a towel around his neck, his eyes are closed, and he is listening to a Sony Walkman. He's dark, good-looking, and he wears bright red swim trunks.

A Young Woman in her 20's enters, carrying textbooks, a pen and a notepad. She is very pretty, but there is something severe about her expression and her manner. She also wears a swimsuit.

As the woman drapes her towel over the sauna rack to dry, the young man opens his eyes and sees her. He stares. The instant she turns around to sit, he shuts his eyes again. She sits at the other end of the sauna, and begins to do what looks like homework. After a few seconds, the young man begins to sing (badly), drawing out syllables as if he were a black soul-man.

MAN. "Let me WRAP you in my WARM and TENder LUH-uhhhh-ove— *(He repeats the phrase. She looks up from her work, not sure what to do about this.)*

WOMAN. Excuse me— *(He hasn't heard her. She leans over and taps him on the shoulder with her pen.)*

MAN. "Said I got to WRAP you in my WARM and— *(She taps him harder. He opens his eyes and slips the headphones onto the back of his head. He pretends to be puzzled.)* Yes?

WOMAN. *(Quite serious.)* Please don't sing. *(She has a Russian accent, which amuses him. But he can't quite place it.)*

MAN. Hey, say that again.

WOMAN. I have said it already once.

MAN. Are you angry?

WOMAN. I am not angry, I am not anything, I just am asking you not to sing.

MAN. *(Still amused.)* You ever hear the expression "It's a free country"?

WOMAN. Yes, I know all about it, but that doesn't mean people should ... should ... should just BURST into song whenever they get this — this —

MAN. Urge?

WOMAN. What is that ... "urge"?

MAN. Desire.

WOMAN. Desire, yes, thank you.

MAN. My pleasure. *(He smiles at her. Uncomfortable, she goes back to work. He watches her, taking off his earphones and shutting off the Walkman.)* What are you? You're Russian, right? *(Beat.)* Right?

WOMAN. *(Not looking up.)* It is a free country, so maybe I choose not to answer you. *(Beat.)* I am from Russia, yes.

MAN. That's what I thought. The way you said: *(Imitating her.)* "Please — don't — sing." *(Tapping his ear.)* I got the ear. Some people got the ear. It's a gift. I don't question it. *(Suddenly.)* Whoa! Wait a minute! You say you're *from* Russia? You mean you actually came over here *from* Russia? In other words, what you're saying to me is, you actually grew up over there? Is that right?

WOMAN. *(Trying to get back to work.)* Yes. Yes. Yes. And yes.

MAN. You been here long or what?

WOMAN. 2 years.

MAN. 2 years. Wow. So like, do you miss it, or what?

WOMAN. Please. Why do you ask me so many questions?

MAN. O.K. You wanna know why? I'll tell you why. I seen you here a couple times, doin' bench presses in the other room there, wondered who you were, wondered what your particular background might be, but I never had no chance to converse with you, and I'm basically what you call a shy-type person, I'm not the kind of person who's gonna come over to a beautiful woman when she's doin' bench presses and presume to introduce himself, but I figured one of these days the opportunity's gonna present itself for the two of us to get acquainted, and when it does —

WOMAN. Yes, yes, enough already. *Please.*

MAN. You sound angry.

WOMAN. I am telling you again I am not angry.

MAN. Hey, great. That makes two of us who ain't angry.

WOMAN. But maybe very soon this could change.

MAN. Call me Vinnie.

WOMAN. Why? Why should I do this?

VINNIE. Gee, I dunno. It seemed like a good idea. *(Beat.)* 'Cause it's my *name.*

WOMAN. I do not understand you at all.

VINNIE. You don't have to apologize. Lots of people've told me I'm a very deep person.

WOMAN. I am not apologizing!

VINNIE. And what may I call you? If I may be so bold to ask and I am?

WOMAN. If you must call me anything, although I do not know why, you may call me Elena.

VINNIE. I like it, I like it— *(Beat.)* So, uh, Elena, you miss it? Russia?

ELENA. No.

VINNIE. Yeah, I hear it's rough over there. I never been there myself. *(Beat.)* So what are you? A student?

ELENA. No. *(She hands him one of her books. He examines it.)*

VINNIE. Oh, you're one of them computer programmers, huh? Very nice. *(Flipping through book.)* That's very popular over here, you know. Very popular profession. *(He hands back her book. She goes back to her work.)* You hate it, right?

ELENA. I do not hate it. I do not love it. I just *do* it.

VINNIE. Yeah, well, you hang in there, something else'll

45

turn up.

ELENA. I don't know anything about that. I just do it. *(Pause.)*

VINNIE. You haven't made a lot of friends here, have you? *(Beat.)* Have you?

ELENA. How did you know that?

VINNIE. O.K. You wanna know how I knew that? I'll tell you how I knew that. 'Cause it suddenly occurs to me: if I am annoying this beautiful young woman so much, how come — I'm askin' myself — she don't just get up and leave? And then, just like that, I remember that every time I seen you here, you never seem to be talkin' to anybody.

ELENA. ...oh. *(Beat.)*

VINNIE. Elena, you into music? You like music?

ELENA. Some. I don't know. Some.

VINNIE. Question: do they have rock and roll in Russia?

ELENA. Some. But to buy the records is for most people very expensive.

VINNIE. So, I guess what I mean is, what do you listen to on the radio?

ELENA. No, you do not understand. If you want to listen to music, you go mainly to other people's apartments and listen to their records.

VINNIE. You mean, it's not like you're walkin' down the street and you hear music comin' from all the different radios in all the cars? It's not like that?

ELENA. Oh no. No, no. Nothing like that.

VINNIE. That's rough, that's rough.

ELENA. I don't know. I don't know is it rough or not. That is just the way it is.

VINNIE. Do they have soul music in Russia?

ELENA. No. What is that? Is this the last question?

VINNIE. Soul music is what I was singing before. It's music you sing from your soul.

ELENA. You are not going to sing again, are you?

VINNIE. Not if you don't want me to, no.

ELENA. I don't want you to.

VINNIE. *(Handing her cassette.)* Now this here in my opinion is a fantastic tape. I inherited all these real old records and tapes from my brother, Sal. What a collection. Out of this world. Listen. *(Before she can protest, he holds one end of the earphones up to her ear, and turns on the Sony. He half-whispers, half-sings the words she is hearing.)* "Let me WRAP you in my WARM and TENder LUH-uhhh-ove—" *(He switches off machine.)* Now just think about those words for a second. This guy, Percy Sledge, this black dude, is singin' about his love — which is a spiritual thing, right? Like it's this — this *overcoat* that he can just take off and *wrap* his girlfriend in — think about that. Just let that sink into your brain for a second or two.

ELENA. *(Handing back tape.)* Very nice.

VINNIE. *(Letting it sink in.)* What a concept. *(Beat.)* Now this music, this goes back, oh, 15 years, maybe more—

ELENA. *(Gathering up her things.)* Yes. Very nice, very nice.

VINNIE. See, back then, according to my brother, Sal, people had real intense emotions about things— *(She is standing, waiting for an opening to leave.)* Now you take Sal for example. He bought the farm, gonna be 2 years next spring—

ELENA. Very nice, yes, uh-huh.

VINNIE. No, that means he died.

ELENA. Yes, sure.

VINNIE. Hey, that's what it means.

ELENA. *(Sees he's serious.)* Please, I'm sorry.

VINNIE. O.K. Never mind. And you wanna know *how* my brother died? I'll tell you how my brother died. He went chasin' after his ex-wife, Loretta, on his motorcycle. All right? He had a vision — Sal told this to one of his buddies at the factory — he had a vision that he could win her back, that he could win back her love. He spent that whole last day, before goin' in to work, playin' all this music he had. Who knows? Maybe this very tape right here, Elena. All right? And that night, he tells his buddy

47

that the music had made him feel like he was bein' born all over again, had made my brother feel that *anything was possible.* Now just think about that for a minute. *(Beat — quick.)* So Sal gets off his job at the factory one midnight, hops on his old beat-up Harley, and blasts off in a cloud of dust on the trail of his ex-, Loretta, who had re-married, but who he knows in his heart still loves him. Ridin' like a madman, my brother, a million stars in the sky lookin' down on him, flashin' off that gold ear-ring he wore, his pony-tail tied up with a rubber-band flappin' in the wind, ridin', ridin' all night long. And then, Elena, just as the sun is comin' up over this hill: Ka-Boom! Never even saw the truck, that's what they told us. Sun blinded him. He was ridin' right into it, Sal was. As fast as that old Harley could carry him. Like he was gonna come out again on the other side. Into the sun. Right into it. *(Beat.)* I still have dreams about it sometimes. Only in the dreams, I'm him. *(Beat.)* But I'll tell you one thing. That's how he woulda wanted it to end. That I know. *(Beat.)* This man had real passion, understand?

ELENA. But—

VINNIE. What?

ELENA. But ... what happened to your brother ... it's horrible.

VINNIE. You don't understand—

ELENA. No! I do understand, I do! Because wherever I go here, that is all I see! This passion! People yelling and beeping their horns and playing their radios. And the way people come up to you and say the first thing that pops into their mouths and the way the men and women are always *looking* at one an-other—

VINNIE. Accordin' to Sal, this ain't nothin'. Years ago, things used to be, like, *really* intense. That's what he told me.

ELENA. No, it is too much. Too much just the way it is.

VINNIE. Accordin' to Sal, there used to be so much passion in this country that people *literally could not stand it.* People used to get all these feelings *without warning* and they didn't know what to do with 'em. Scared the hell out of everybody.

ELENA. Good for them. I don't blame them one bit.

VINNIE. Why?

ELENA. Why?! Why?! Because you cannot live like that. How can you live like that? That's ... that's crazy!

VINNIE. Hey, don't be angry.

ELENA. I'm not angry! *(Beat.)* I'm sorry, but I guess I just do not understand you at all.

VINNIE. Call me Vinnie.

ELENA. Nothing you have said. Nothing. It makes no sense at all.

VINNIE. Vinnie.

ELENA. You make no sense to me at all, Vinnie.

VINNIE. *(Shaking her hand.)* In that case, may I say that it has been a pleasure makin' your acquaintance, Elena, and I want to leave you with one final thought before we part company for the day. May I do that?

ELENA. I think I have no choice.

VINNIE. *(Confidentially.)* "Anything ... is possible."

ELENA. *(Disengaging her hand.)* Yes. Anything is possible. All right. Whatever you say.

VINNIE. You get down to the Village much?

ELENA. Sometimes.

VINNIE. All right. Sometime, in the near future, we won't set a date, when you're ready, I don't want to rush you, I can see you're the kind of person likes to take things one step at a time, I'd like you to come down to the Paradise Bar, corner of Sullivan and West Third, visit with me, have a couple of drinks, whatever. All drinks, of course, will be on the house.

ELENA. You own this place?

VINNIE. No, no, I tend bar there, every night but Wednesday.

ELENA. Oh.

VINNIE. It's kind of a dump, but it's got class, know what I mean?

ELENA. No, of course I don't know what you mean. I keep telling you this.

VINNIE. The customers are great. A little grungy, maybe, but good people, basically, is what I'm sayin.' You'll like 'em. I'll introduce you. Why not, right? Anyway, you think about it.

ELENA. I think about it.

VINNIE. Hey, that's all I'm askin'.

ELENA. All right, all right, I think about it. *(Opening door.)* Anyway, I will see you here. Yes?

VINNIE. You got it.

ELENA. Got what?

VINNIE. Whatever it is, Elena, you got it.

ELENA. *(Weary.)* Enough for today. Good-bye, Vinnie.

VINNIE. You take care now, Elena. *(She leaves. He sits back, a smile spreading across his face. He puts his headphones back on, and turns on the Sony. He closes his eyes and sings.)* "Let me WRAP you in my WARM and TENder LUH-uhhhh-ove—" *(Maybe one more chorus, then a quick fade.)*

THE END

PROPERTY PLOT

Onstage

Textbooks
Pen
Notepad
Sony Walkman
Towels

SOAP OPERA

SOAP OPERA was originally commissioned by Actors Theatre of Louisville in 1982.

The play should be staged simply, with the actors seated on stools. Each actor should have a separate spotlight. Lucy should be in the middle, with Johnny and Sharon equidistant on either side. The actors should wear the kind of clothes the characters would wear to work.

When Lucy talks, it's as if she were telling her story to a roomful of girlfriends. Johnny treats the audience one-on-one, as if telling his story to a psychiatrist or a confessor. Sharon addresses the audience somewhat didactically, as if she's been invited here to give a lecture.

For Lucy's last section, her relationship to the audience changes. It might be helpful to think of the audience as a mirror in which she's trying to see her own reflection.

The spots on Johnny and Sharon should go off abruptly at the appropriate moments during Lucy's final speech.

The characters are in their mid-twenties. Lucy could be younger than that; Sharon could be older.

The time of the play is the present.

CHARACTERS

Lucy
Johnny
Sharon

SOAP OPERA

LUCY. I can have just about any man I want these days. It's great. But for a long time, I used to think of myself as being unattractive and couldn't get many men at all. I hated that period in my life, and I hated myself too. Until I met this guy, Johnny. Johnny really dug me. He told me he used to think of himself as being unattractive to women, or something like that, and for a long time went around hating himself also. But he was *so* attracted to me that he just threw all his inhibitions right out the window. He pursued me constantly until I agreed to go out with him — he worshipped me — he adored me. I couldn't *believe* that a man was paying this much attention to me. (You have to understand: I was, like, incredibly shy.) *(Beat. She smiles at this memory of herself.)* But Johnny changed all that. He would say things to me, things that an intelligent person would consider sentimental or corny, about my eyes, my lips, my hair. And at first I thought: oh come on, *Jesus* — *(Beat. Very thoughtful.)* But I'll tell you something: when someone really believes what he's saying, you believe it, too. When someone tells you, over and over, that he loves you, that you're the most precious thing in his whole life, you lay awake at night beside him, crying, trying to find within yourself the qualities that he seems able to see so clearly and at last you see them, too. And it's like: *well, of course. (Beat.)* And you know that you can inspire love in a man. *(Beat.)* Or he would say things to me that at first embarrassed me like crazy. Him too, I could tell. But Johnny was just so head over heels in love that embarrassment flew right out the window, and the next thing I know, we're in this dark restaurant. With

55

wine and candlelight. With beautiful thick red napkins spread over our laps. Holding hands under the table. And Johnny's leaning over the flame and whispering things to me about ... my cunt. And he's saying the word: cunt. And I just couldn't *believe* it. He's telling me what he loves about it, how it feels and how it tastes. *(Beat.)* O.K., but you want to know something? When a man talks like that to you, I don't care what your upbringing is, how shocked you are at first, when you can see in his eyes that he really means it, that he's not playing a game, and not trying to be this super-cool stud, you just nearly die with the desire that pours all through you. You just think about him wanting you so much that he can *say* such things to you, and *his* desire for you becomes *your* desire for him. *(Beat.)* Well, by the time the waiter came with our food, I had to keep my head down and bite my lip, because I was trembling so hard. I could feel myself wanting to burst free for the first time in my life, and Johnny, that bastard, just squeezed my hand under the table and smiled. He knew, he knew. *(Beat.)* Oh let me tell you, that was some night. From that night on, the sex between us, which had been good, became *incredible.* Johnny couldn't believe that I had ever considered myself unattractive to men, and for the first time in my life, I couldn't either. And right about then, other guys started to pay attention to me at the office, the same guys who would just shove papers in my tray and tell me to take them to so and so. At first I was baffled, but then I took a good look at myself in the mirror in the ladies' room, and I thought: well, Lucy ... *of course.* Because the face that looked back at me knew two things so clearly that any guy who looked into it would also know it right away and would have to deal with it. And the two things were, one: that I could inspire love in a man, and two: that I could drive that same man mad with physical desire. *(Beat.)* It never ceases to amaze me how when you truly see yourself in a certain way, others see you that way too.

JOHNNY. The thing about Lucy was how she could make me feel like I could say or do anything to her when we were alone.

She could take the whole world and just put it away somewhere, on the other side of the door, and the world didn't matter anymore. The world could not touch us or tell us what to do or make us feel guilty about what we said or what we did. It was just us, only us. And that suited me fine, because what had the world ever done for me but bring me sorrow and pain? I had accepted, long ago, the truth which came with the pain —which are two words for the same thing, as I see it — and this made me different from other people right off, who think that *pain* is one thing and *the truth* another. That's their problem and not mine, although I'm sure they don't see it that way. Most people don't really *see* things at all, because most people are so *stupid* that it never dawns on them what life really is: just a word for something which we are all part of, which doesn't care that *we* are a part of *it*; which doesn't care about our dreams, or give two shits about our chances for finding beauty or happiness. *(Beat.)* When I was 10 years old, I stood in my pajamas in the grass, about an hour before sunrise, and watched our house go up in flames. Through the smoke, the sky was so lovely I could never describe it, filled with soft stars fading into the blue. I thought: it's like another world. Which is a pretty obvious and stupid way of putting it, but I was in shock so they told me, so I guess it was not so stupid after all. Even after the funeral, off by myself at night, all I could think was how impossible the heavens looked, too beautiful to be true, all lit up and quiet and so endless....I wanted to die, in that moment of silence, not like my brother and sisters in the fire, but peacefully, sweetly. I wanted to turn into a vapor, into a mist, and be pulled upward, stretched so thin that there would be nothing left of me, just swirling dust, soft and bright....After a while, I could hear the screaming again, but far away, where it couldn't hurt me. I could hear the roaring of the water in the hoses: it was soothing. It made me smile and feel sleepy. I stood still and closed my eyes and floated away, off the face of this earth. There was a cooler and cooler breeze the higher I got, higher than the birds and the planets, and with my eyes shut tight, I saw it all again, from a heavenly distance: my mother, naked, her body black with soot, held back by neighbors, clawing and digging her fingers into the air like it was a living thing she could rip apart; my father, naked, his arms wrapped around himself, the nails of his fingers digging into the flesh of his sides, his legs rooted to the earth like a tree.... The way he bellowed before he fell to his knees and pitched forward into the earth...into the flowers my mother had planted years before. *(Beat.)* The thing about Lucy, the thing that made me want to fuck her endlessly, that made me want to enter her as no man has ever entered a woman before was how she could take the whole world and just put it away somewhere, and the world didn't matter anymore. And how, with every move our bodies made together in the night, it was only us, it was only us, Lucy and Johnny, Lucy and Johnny, only us.

SHARON. What I liked about Johnny almost immediately was: I could actually *talk* to the man. Occasionally, it's true, people encourage you to talk to them, if they sense something uncontrollable about to burst apart inside you, but the sad fact is that once you start talking they don't really listen, or they *pretend* to listen — out of politeness — but they don't really *hear*, so that whenever you open your mouth, it's like you're terrified you might be wasting another human being's valuable time ... and all the feelings inside you dry up and die. But Johnny you could really talk to. He really listened. *(Beat.)* I used to be able to talk to Lisa, of course, up to about 6 months before she moved out and said those things to me I won't ever forget, or forgive her for saying. Lisa had been my third lover — female, that is — our affair lasting nearly 2 years. It'd been quite a while since I'd been involved sexually with a man, although the chemical attraction, in my case, never entirely disappeared. But on those rare occasions when I'd feel, if you'll pardon the expression, *aroused*, I'd just remember the way it had been between myself and men, and the moment would pass. There's this ... dimension ... which a woman can share with another woman, which she just can't with most men, and once you've experienced *that* kind of intimacy, an intimacy you dreamed about since you were a little girl but thought was impossible — *(Beat. She wants to make this clear and simple, but she's at a loss for words.)* Your soul — *(She smiles.)* — sings! *(She laughs.)* Well, I'm sorry, that's the only way I can express it. I mean ... you go to sleep cradled in her arms, and you can hear it, quietly, inside you [I swear this is true]. You wake up in the morning, and one of you is making breakfast for the other, and you can still hear it. Only now it seems to be coming from *her*, not you. It's very confusing and very funny, and what's *really* con fusing is if it's your first time with a woman, it takes a while before you realize she's experiencing *exactly* the same confusion as you — only she knows how to relax and enjoy it — and the funniest thing of all is that no matter where you are, no matter where *she* is, whether the two of you are in each other's arms or one of you is hundreds of miles away ... *(Beat. This makes her smile again.)* ... the singing ... never ... quite ... stops. *(Beat.)* I met Johnny one afternoon in late May in Central Park. I was supposed to be doing some preliminary sketches for a painting I'd been commissioned to — but that's not important. What's important was this beautiful man, sitting on a rock, his knees up to his chin, staring off into the distance. There was a grease spot on his T-shirt which just looked *so* right. It took a long time before he noticed me staring at him. He was supposed to meet his girlfriend here on her lunch break. She worked in an office nearby. Johnny didn't start work until 4: he was a mechanic at one of those around-the-clock gas stations on 10th avenue near the tunnel. The so-called girlfriend, Lucy, *never* showed up. *(Beat.)* Right then, without ever having met her or anything, I just *knew* she was a bitch.

LUCY. For the first few months, I had no problem turning down dates with the guys in my office, because everything was still going hot and heavy between me and Johnny. Besides,

these guys had never deigned to give me the time of day before, so my feeling was: eat your hearts out, you assholes. Of course, I only said this in my mind. In actuality, I would always smile sweetly as I brought in some paperwork, you know, and pretend not to notice the bulges in their trousers. One day, as we were waiting in line for the morning coffee, Tom Jergens expressed his carnal appetite for me in no uncertain terms. [Yes, he actually referred to it as his "carnal appetite". Some men really are assholes; there is just no question about it.] "You are so ... self-assured these past few months, Luce," he said. "You're like a new person. You're driving me fucking crazy, you know that?" Well, naturally I knew that, but all I said was:"Why, thank you, Tom." And smiling sweetly, I walked back to my desk. *(Beat.)* Once, when I told Johnny I had to spend the night with my sick mother, I went home with Tom. He was a good-looking guy and it was fun balling him, but it was nothing special, and I told him so. In a nice way, of course. The expression on his face when I told him was just incredible. *(Beat.)* So from time to time, say every other week, even though I was still with Johnny, I would sort of treat myself to one of these men at the office. For someone like myself, who had once considered herself unattractive and been shit on and humiliated because of it, it was a really educational experience. I never realized how screwed up most men were in bed, how many doubts they had about themselves, how desperately they needed the approval of a woman, especially a woman as self-assured and confident as I had become. Really, it was just too hysterical. I dreamed about writing my own advice column, like Dr. Joyce Brothers, except I would be a lot more down-to-earth than her. I dreamed about telling the whole truth and no holds barred. The whole truth and nothing but the truth about men and women so help me God as long as we all shall live. *(Beat.)* Power. It's a beautiful thing.
JOHNNY. The day that Lucy didn't show up in the park was the day I met this lady, Sharon. Which was a good thing, I guess, because it took my mind off Lucy and wondering what the hell

60

could have happened to her. Sharon wanted to do my picture. "Me?!" I said. She thought that was funny, the look on my face when I said that. *(Beat.)* All the while she was sketching my picture, she talked. And talked ... and talked! I decided she was one of those people who has to let everybody know what is going on inside of them — as though it really matters to somebody else what's going on inside of *you* — and that that was maybe why this lover of hers had finally decided to move out on her, because it was my guess that she had just never stopped talking, which would be enough to drive most men crazy. But even though this thought was in my head, I didn't reveal it to her. The truth is, even if I had wanted to, it would've been impossible because she was talking so much that ... *(Beat.)* The truth is I liked the sound of her voice. I thought it was ... lovely. I closed my eyes to hear it better, and for a while everything stopped for me. There was only the wind in the treetops and the hot sunlight on my face and the faraway sound of her voice. *(Beat.)* I opened my eyes and felt this strange desire to tell her things. I don't mean I wasn't listening to what she was saying, because I was, but I was also aware of myself filling up with all kinds of things I wanted to tell her. Things that I had never told Lucy. Private things. I couldn't understand where this desire was coming from, but it was very intense. With Lucy, I would tell her just enough and no more, and that was how we both liked it. Lucy would look up into my eyes as I slipped inside her and she would see that there were secrets inside me, dark secrets, that she would never know, that I would never reveal to her, ever, and that excited her. I would spread her arms far apart on the bed and hold them down with all my strength so that she couldn't move them, no matter how hard she tried or cried out. *(Beat.)* But this was different. *(Beat.)* When she was finished, Sharon showed me the picture. All I could think was: is that me? Because, honestly, it didn't resemble me at all. But the more I stared at it, the more I saw that it did. It was as though I was seeing into my face for the first time. At the garage where I

61

worked, maybe 50 times a night I would pass by the cigarette machine with the mirror set into it, and I would sneak a look at myself on the run, but this wasn't the same thing at all. This was different. Damn! She was smiling at me when I finally looked up from the picture, but all I could think was: how did you do that?!

SHARON. As I said, the thing I liked about Johnny almost immediately was that I could really talk to him. Ever since Lisa moved out, I'd been storing up all this emotion inside me, waiting for some poor unsuspecting soul to come along and be my captive audience of one: and now *here he was*. God, yes, this is perfect, I thought, thank you so much. I can keep talking my heart out forever and this lovely man with the beautiful grease stain on his T-shirt will just keep sitting on that rock and let me. *(Beat.)* The sketch wasn't particularly good, but he loved it. He didn't say that; he didn't *have* to say that. His eyes said it all, like a child's, when he looked up from the drawing and smiled at me. It was as though I'd captured something inside of him that nobody else had even guessed was there, and he couldn't figure out how I'd done it. There was such tenderness and strength in his voice when he thanked me for the picture that I became afraid suddenly, afraid that, perhaps, I was merely *imagining* the depth of his feeling ... because ... because, dammit, it was certainly true that I *was* in need of someone who could — what I *mean* is, it was not unlike me to imbue other people, *on occasion,* with qualities that I desperately wanted them to have. But what if what I thought I sensed in him *was* real? I wondered immediately how he'd react if he knew that the lover I'd mentioned was a woman. Would that bother him? And why hadn't I told him in the first place?....And why the hell were thoughts like this even coming into my head? Dammit, this was crazy! This was just a lovely man sunning himself in the park on a spring day and staring mysteriously off into the distance. He had nothing whatsoever to do with my life, *nothing*, any more than the thousands and thousands of people we pass on the street each day without a second thought have anything to do with the secret world of our dreams, or we with theirs. *(Beat.)* I suggested we meet again in a few days. Same place, same time. Johnny said O.K. *(Beat.)* After he left to go to his job, I wandered through the park. God, it was such a beautiful day! I could actually feel my thoughts becoming one with the life around me: with the wind high up in the trees; with the birds — in sudden flight — disappearing into the sun. Then, like some goddamn black cloud out of nowhere, an old fear passed over me, and there was absolutely nothing I could do about it. Except, of course, to let it have its way with me. *(Beat.)* See, it's like this: I think that what you look for in another person, finally, is something ... which lets you know this person will go the distance with you. That they will be there for you, that they will not collapse when you ... need all their strength. And of course you silently make the same promise to be there for them ... to go the distance. *(Beat.)* But you just never know. *(Beat.)* I have watched people over the years, people whose strength and self-assurance and intellectual gifts were remarkable ... just fall apart. It doesn't seem to matter who you are: rich or poor, sick or healthy, someone or no one. You never know when the bottom is going to drop out of your life. Or theirs. *(Beat. She laughs.)* How exciting, you know? *(Beat.)* Anyway, like it always did, the fear left me after a while and the real world took its place. I stretched out in the cool grass and kicked off my sandals and looked up at the sky. God, but it was lovely: not a fucking cloud in sight.

LUCY. I can remember the exact moment when I saw Johnny for what he really was. Believe me, it was like being hit with a ton of bricks. What happened was I stood him up for this date we were supposed to have in the park — I had made a date with this other guy in the meantime — and when Johnny called me up later at work and bought the really lame excuse I gave him, I distinctly remember this voice inside my head whispering: Hey, Lucy. This guy is *pathetic.* Doesn't he even suspect by now that you've been cheating on him? *(Beat.)* Believe it or not, that was the first moment when I faced the truth: that it was all over. Like, *finito*. Admit it, Lucy, I said to myself in the mirror of the ladies' room, Johnny is *weak*. He is so dependant on you for his strength that he's afraid to admit that maybe you're losing interest in him. Wow, I thought, that's right, that's right: he's *afraid*! I was absolutely *amazed* that this had never occurred to me before. He's afraid to even think about what would happen if he had to live in the *real* world of men and women. Because Johnny had said when I first met him how he had always had, like, these problems with women, and at the time I dug him so much for saying that because I thought: aw, hey, this guy's just like me. Which is to say that all he lacked was confidence in himself as a person. Or, to put it another way, he did not know who he really was as a man, just like I did not know who I really was as a woman. And so we could start from scratch, the two of us, and find out together. And because it had been so great at first, which is to say the romance I had always dreamed of, and the incredible sex I had always dreamed of, all coming together at the same time, I had failed to pay attention to what was *really* happening, namely, that I had come to know who I was as a woman, but poor Johnny still didn't have a clue who he was as a man. Wow, I said to myself in the mirror, and it took you this long to figure it all out: talk about *naive. (Beat.)* Well, the *more* I thought about it, the more unhealthy our relationship seemed to me. It was like Johnny needed to feel that we were the only two people in the world or something when we were making love, which I used to think was romantic. But now — in a flash! — I saw it for the sickness it really was. And no *wonder* he always had problems with women: I mean, the way he would stare at *me* sometimes, with those creepy eyes of his, so serious and all, it would be enough to make any healthy woman think twice about the guy. It was like he had this screwy vision of life locked up inside him that you couldn't ask him about — no, of course not, because *he* wouldn't let you! — which made him superior to everybody else — in his own twisted way of thinking, of course! — and when you were with him you had to give yourself up to this ... force or whatever it was and — well, fuck that, sweetheart! *(Beat.)* God, I was mad! I thought about him wanting me so much that he had made me deny and nearly *forget* all about myself — about *myself* — about the real person I was always meant to be ... and suddenly *his* desire for me became my ... my *loathing* for him. *(Beat.)* But I wasn't ready for a scene just yet. Oh, no. My vacation started in a few days and I had made plans to spend two weeks in Atlantic City with this young lawyer who had moved into my building. After I was all rested up and all, with a super-tan to boot, *then* when I came back, *then* I would tell Johnny it was all over. *Then* I would put an end to this sordid chapter in my life and move on to the next one. *(Beat.)* Suddenly, there was this voice inside me, whispering: But he loves you, Lucy. Johnny *loves* you....I looked back at myself in the ladies' room mirror and I said: Look, that is *his* problem and not mine. *(Beat.)* Well...*of course.*

SHARON. During the two weeks when this so-called girl-friend of his was on vacation, Johnny and I spent a great deal of time together. There was nothing physical between us, but I began to feel so certain that there would be, that I stopped worrying about it. Slowly, we opened up to each other. *Nothing* like this had happened to me since my first year with Lisa — I still hadn't told him about her or the other women in my life, but now I knew I would. I just didn't know when. *(Beat.)* He told me things he had never told anyone before, about the tragedy he'd experienced when he was 10 and how he'd never gotten over it. How it had stamped him as different from everyone else — in his own mind — and created all these problems for him....Because he couldn't bring himself to talk about his feelings, people often got the wrong idea. Women, especially, found him cold and mysterious and withdrawn. And more and more, the world seemed to him a place in which he just didn't belong. Maybe, he started to reason, none of us could say we really belonged here, on this Earth, *at all*; not the way the trees belonged, certainly, or the grass or the wind. The weather inside us — these were *his* words — was always changing and making us crazy. Like, he said, when snow sometimes starts falling in May, and all at once the seasons don't seem to make sense anymore, and how you could *see* this on peoples' faces: that they just didn't know where they were — like that, he said.... He used to dream about what life would be like if human beings could only know who they *really* were and why they were *here*, and how, he said, all you would need to do then, see, all anyone would need to do, if they got confused or forgot, would be to *look* at someone, and the meaning they were searching for would be there, in that other person's eyes. *(Beat. She laughs.)* Just your normal everyday kind of conversation, right? *(Beat.)* I really liked the guy. What can I say?

JOHNNY. I couldn't help wondering if Lucy would notice this big change in me that Sharon kept talking about. She said it was like something had relaxed inside of me, and that she could *see* it in my face. To be honest, I couldn't see it for myself, but I believed her, because I felt it. I just didn't know what to call it. *(Beat.)* I guess I would have believed whatever Sharon told me. She was just so much more intelligent than anyone I had ever met, how could I *not* believe her? .... I really wanted to understand *everything* Sharon talked to me about, and I think I did ... except for this dream of hers that she described to me. I could tell there was supposed to be more than one meaning to it and that she wanted me to discover it by myself, without telling me, but I just couldn't piece it out. *(Beat.)* In her dream it was afternoon. Indian summer, she said. She was standing at the corner of 42nd Street and 9th Avenue where they've got all these new theatres now, with colored banners hanging out front. And everywhere she looked there were couples, holding hands and laughing while they walked, the breeze off the Hudson lifting the ladies' dresses and blowing the men's ties back over their shoulders and rearranging everyone's hair styles. And the particles of dust flying around kept getting into everyone's eyes but no one seemed to mind. And the bits of mica in the sidewalk reflected the sun everywhere you looked so that you could barely see. And the red and blue and yellow banners were flapping like crazy, and it was wonderful, she said, like being inside a kaleidescope, with everything moving around you and changing. *(Beat.)* Then this really strange thing happened. The couples stopped walking, and each couple joined hands with the next couple and so on, until everyone was linked together in this endless chain ... and the men began turning into women ... and the women began turning into men, and everyone was turning into someone else, until, she said, it just didn't seem to matter anymore, it just didn't matter that you couldn't say for certain that *there* was a man or *there* was a woman, and it was the first time, she said, that she had witnessed something beautiful which also made her laugh. *(Beat.)* Understand? she said. No, I said, not really. But she said that was all right, that the next time we got together there was something she wanted to tell me about, this person she wanted to tell me about, and when she did, maybe then I would understand. I said anything she wanted to tell me was fine with me. *(Beat.)* That night I went to work at the station. Tomorrow Lucy would be coming back from her vacation and it was all I could do to control my ... *happiness* I guess you'd call it, over her coming back, over my relationship with Sharon ... over everything. *(Beat.)* I took a break from this transmission I was fooling with and went outside. There were these long silver clouds moving like ships across the sky. You could see the stars through them, and the moon. And these clouds, Jesus, they were *flying*. I could imagine them travelling around and around the Earth, never stopping.... I had a tremendous sense of motion, of myself in motion, and of being part of something so much bigger than myself it hurt just to think about it. *(Beat.)* I went to Lucy's apartment early the next day and opened it with my key. I wanted to be there when she got back so I could surprise her. *(Beat.)* After about an hour, I heard laughing out in the hall. Then Lucy came in with this guy.

They were both carrying suitcases. When she saw me, she told him he'd better leave and she would talk to him later. Then she slammed the door and started yelling at me. Where the fuck did I get off, she said, letting myself into her apartment when she wasn't there? It was over, she said, it was all over! It'd been over a long time ago so far as she was concerned. Didn't I realize that? she said. Was I fucking stupid or what? I didn't remember the other things she said, I just stood there watching her screaming at me, but I couldn't hear the words anymore, it was like I was watching some character on TV with the sound turned off. Then everything in the room started moving around and around me and my legs started shaking and it was like my body didn't know how to hold itself upright anymore, and then the sound came back on and she was yelling at me to get out, to get out and never come back and when I didn't move she came closer to me and said what's the matter, didn't I hear what she said, was I fucking deaf or something? Get out, she said, get out get out get out get out! She opened the door and pushed me out into the hall and slammed the door behind her and the next sound I heard was brakes screeching from somewhere and then there was this guy leaning out the window of a car and blowing his horn at me and yelling at me to get the fuck out of the street and to look where the fuck I was going and I just stared at him as he drove off, giving me the finger, and I walked away and kept on walking.

SHARON. There was a knocking on my door, just as I was getting ready to go out for the afternoon. It was Johnny. Something terrible must've happened to him from the look on his face, but he wouldn't tell me what it was. Suddenly, he grabbed me and pulled me to him and started kissing me and forcing me down onto the floor, and I yelled at him to stop and tried to push him away, but he took my arms and spread them out and held them down so I couldn't move. He tried to kiss me again, but I kept twisting my head away and then I started crying and couldn't stop, and finally I felt him let go of me and stand up.

(Beat.) I couldn't stop crying, no matter how hard I tried. He covered his mouth with his hand and kept backing away until his body came up against the wall and slowly moved down the length of it, and he stayed like that, his knees up to his chin, staring past me and shaking his head from side to side. He kept saying he was sorry, he was sorry. Then he stood up and ran to the door and he was gone. It was minutes before I could even sit up and figure out what had happened to him, and then suddenly I knew, and I also knew where he had to be going. He'd told me once where she lived and I grabbed for the telephone book — but I couldn't remember her last name. It was almost an hour later before it came to me. I looked it up and found the address and wrote it down. *(Beat.)* When I got to her apartment, I could hear voices inside. One of them was Johnny's. I tried the door. It was unlocked.

LUCY. I heard the key turning in the lock and it was Johnny again. He came inside and reached into his jacket before I could say anything. And pulled out this gun. There was a pricetag dangling from it. He said he was going to kill me. He said that he loved me. I tried to get him to put the gun away but I don't remember what I said, or how long we stood there. I just remember him raising the gun and then suddenly the door behind him opening and the woman coming in and running to him and screaming and the look in his eyes when he saw her and the look in her eyes when he shot her... again and again and again... and then his pulling me to him so gently and crying and touching my hair all over and my face and my lips and telling me he loved me, he would always love me. Forever. *(Beat.)* And putting the gun into his mouth and squeezing the trigger. *(Pause.)* That was a year ago. I moved out of my apartment and took another one in a different part of town. I still have trouble sleeping. *(Beat.)* You read about such things in the paper, you see those awful headlines in the *Post*, but you don't think it can ever happen to you. You have to put it out of your mind, that's the only thing you can do. You have to pretend it happened to

69

somebody else, not you, and you have to make yourself forget about it, just like you forget about yesterday's news. *(Beat.)* I put it out of my mind and went on with my life. You have to. *(Beat.)* I joined a health club. *(Beat.)* And I have a new boyfriend. *(Beat.)* The doctors say I've made a complete recovery, and I know it's true, and I'm proud of that. Lots of people, Lucy, they told me, would be scarred by something like this for the rest of their lives. That made me feel good when they said that. You have to be strong, they said. You *are* strong, they said. Just keep telling yourself that. *(Beat.)* I do. Each and every day. *(Beat.)* But I went to this restaurant with my boyfriend not long ago. It reminded me of the place Johnny used to take me way back when, and I guess that's why I started having these thoughts. I wondered if what happened to Johnny could happen to him, I mean could he just wake up one day and not be living in the real world anymore, and not even know it? I got this chill: could something like that ever happen to me? *(Beat.)* There's just no point in even thinking about such things. *(Beat.)* Last night I dreamed about Johnny. About when we first met and he made me feel something about myself that I had never felt before. *(Beat.)* Maybe I should've tried to love him back then. Maybe everything would've turned out different if I'd at least tried, but — *(Suddenly she desperately needs to explain this.)* — it just never really occurred to me ... *(Almost pleading.)* ... you know??

(Fade Out.)

THE END

PROPERTY PLOT

Onstage

3 stools

NEW PLAYS

★ **SHEL'S SHORTS by Shel Silverstein.** Lauded poet, songwriter and author of children's books, the incomparable Shel Silverstein's short plays are deeply infused with the same wicked sense of humor that made him famous. "...[a] childlike honesty and twisted sense of humor." *–Boston Herald.* "...terse dialogue and an absurdity laced with a tang of dread give [*Shel's Shorts*] more than a trace of Samuel Beckett's comic existentialism." *–Boston Phoenix.* [flexible casting] ISBN: 0-8222-1897-6

★ **AN ADULT EVENING OF SHEL SILVERSTEIN by Shel Silverstein.** Welcome to the darkly comic world of Shel Silverstein, a world where nothing is as it seems and where the most innocent conversation can turn menacing in an instant. These ten imaginative plays vary widely in content, but the style is unmistakable. "...[*An Adult Evening*] shows off Silverstein's virtuosic gift for wordplay...[and] sends the audience out...with a clear appreciation of human nature as perverse and laughable." *–NY Times.* [flexible casting] ISBN: 0-8222-1873-9

★ **WHERE'S MY MONEY? by John Patrick Shanley.** A caustic and sardonic vivisection of the institution of marriage, laced with the author's inimitable razor-sharp wit. "...Shanley's gift for acid-laced one-liners and emotionally tumescent exchanges is certainly potent..." *–Variety.* "...lively, smart, occasionally scary and rich in reverse wisdom." *–NY Times.* [3M, 3W] ISBN: 0-8222-1865-8

★ **A FEW STOUT INDIVIDUALS by John Guare.** A wonderfully screwy comedy-drama that figures Ulysses S. Grant in the throes of writing his memoirs, surrounded by a cast of fantastical characters, including the Emperor and Empress of Japan, the opera star Adelina Patti and Mark Twain. "Guare's smarts, passion and creativity skyrocket to awesome heights..." *–Star Ledger.* "...precisely the kind of good new play that you might call an everyday miracle...every minute of it is fresh and newly alive..." *–Village Voice.* [10M, 3W] ISBN: 0-8222-1907-7

★ **BREATH, BOOM by Kia Corthron.** A look at fourteen years in the life of Prix, a Bronx native, from her ruthless girl-gang leadership at sixteen through her coming to maturity at thirty. "...vivid world, believable and eye-opening, a place worthy of a dramatic visit, where no one would want to live but many have to." *–NY Times.* "...rich with humor, terse vernacular strength and gritty detail..." *–Variety.* [1M, 9W] ISBN: 0-8222-1849-6

★ **THE LATE HENRY MOSS by Sam Shepard.** Two antagonistic brothers, Ray and Earl, are brought together after their father, Henry Moss, is found dead in his seedy New Mexico home in this classic Shepard tale. "...His singular gift has been for building mysteries out of the ordinary ingredients of American family life..." *–NY Times.* "...rich moments ...Shepard finds gold." *–LA Times.* [7M, 1W] ISBN: 0-8222-1858-5

★ **THE CARPETBAGGER'S CHILDREN by Horton Foote.** One family's history spanning from the Civil War to WWII is recounted by three sisters in evocative, intertwining monologues. "...bittersweet music—[a] rhapsody of ambivalence...in its modest, garrulous way...theatrically daring." *–The New Yorker.* [3W] ISBN: 0-8222-1843-7

★ **THE NINA VARIATIONS by Steven Dietz.** In this funny, fierce and heartbreaking homage to *The Seagull*, Dietz puts Chekhov's star-crossed lovers in a room and doesn't let them out. "A perfect little jewel of a play..." *–Shepherdstown Chronicle.* "...a delightful revelation of a writer at play; and also an odd, haunting, moving theater piece of lingering beauty." *–Eastside Journal (Seattle).* [1M, 1W (flexible casting)] ISBN: 0-8222-1891-7

DRAMATISTS PLAY SERVICE, INC.
440 Park Avenue South, New York, NY 10016 212-683-8960 Fax 212-213-1539
postmaster@dramatists.com www.dramatists.com